DATE DUE

4			

DEMCO 38-297

The Story of
FORT SUMTER

by Eugenia Burney

illustrated by Chuck Mitchell

CHILDRENS PRESS, CHICAGO

Library of Congress Cataloging in Publication Data

Burney, Eugenia.
 Fort Sumter.

 (Cornerstones of freedom)
  SUMMARY: Discusses the people and events at Fort
Sumter, South Carolina during the Civil War period.
  [1. Sumter, Fort—Fiction] I. Mitchell, Chuck, ill.
II. Title.
PZ7.B93415Fo   [Fic]   74-28435
ISBN 0-516-04611-X

8 9 10 11 R 93 92 91 90

"Get out of here, you old cow!" Danny Sinclair shouted as he helped Captain Abner Doubleday chase the animal over the eroded walls of Fort Moultrie.

Captain Doubleday stopped on top of the wall and looked toward Charleston, South Carolina. Then he looked seaward to Fort Sumter where a crew of laborers worked on the fortifications.

Danny's father was the sutler, a man who bought provisions for the garrison. His family lived in Fort Moultrie along with the soldiers and their families. Danny admired tall, handsome Captain Doubleday who had taught the boys a new ball game which he had invented. They called it baseball.

"How long will it take to finish Fort Sumter?" Danny asked.

"Too long," Captain Doubleday answered. "If Abraham Lincoln is elected President South Carolina will secede from the Union and other states will follow her."

"I don't know what that means," Danny said.

Captain Doubleday tried to explain.

"Ever since the thirteen colonies won the Revolutionary War they have called themselves the United States of America. They have one government with one president in Washington.

"The people who live in the southern states farm big plantations that need hundreds of black slaves. The people who live in the northern states manufacture cloth and shoes and trade with other countries by ship."

Danny nodded.

"Many people in the northern states believe that slavery is wrong. They say the people in the southern states should free their slaves," Captain Doubleday went on. "But the Southerners cannot run their plantations without slaves. They have decided that they will withdraw from the United States and form their own government. The Northerners say they can't do that."

"I don't know which is right," Danny said.

"No one really knows," the captain said grimly, "but men on both sides are willing to fight for what they believe is right."

The captain was worried about what would happen to the men at Fort Moultrie. If a stray cow could walk over the sand-covered walls, it would be easy enough for men to do the same thing.

Fort Sumter was another matter. More than thirty years earlier army engineers began making an artificial island on a shoal in Charleston Harbor.

The large pentagon-shaped fort was one of the strongest in the United States. The three-storied brick shell was completed but the guns were not mounted. It was named for Thomas Sumter, the famous South Carolina general of the Revolutionary War.

"Why doesn't the president send some more men?" Danny asked.

"Major Anderson has asked for reinforcements nearly every day since he arrived four weeks ago," Captain Doubleday said, "but President Buchanan thinks they would make the Southerners more angry."

Major Robert Anderson, like Captain Doubleday, was a graduate of West Point. He was a Southerner and could understand how the South Carolinians felt. Their grandfathers had defended Fort Moultrie in the Revolutionary War and it belonged to them. They would take it any time they chose.

In November Abraham Lincoln was elected President of the United States. The South Carolina Convention met in Charleston in December and unanimously voted for secession.

The citizens of Charleston went wild. People ran up and down the streets, laughing and crying. They rang bells, fired cannon, and set fire to barrels of tar.

Major Anderson had no orders to move to Fort Sumter, but Secretary of War John Floyd had written him that if he was afraid of an attack on Fort Moultrie he could move to Fort Sumter. Major Anderson believed that South Carolina's secession would bring an attack. He decided to move soon but he did not dare tell anyone.

Every evening, just after dark, two South Carolina boats patrolled the water between Fort Moultrie and Fort Sumter. Major Anderson planned to take his men over after the sun went down but before the boats began to patrol.

On the day after Christmas he ordered Lieutenant Norman Hall to gather the women and children on the parade ground.

"I am afraid Fort Moultrie may be attacked," the Major told them. "I am going to send you to Fort Johnson where you will be safe."

Danny Sinclair was disappointed but he went with his mother and brother in one of the two boats. Instead of going all the way to Fort Johnson, however, Lieutenant Hall stopped the boats in the water just beyond Fort Sumter. Major Anderson had secretly told Lieutenant Hall to wait there until he heard two guns fired at Fort Moultrie. This signal would mean that the garrison was safely at Fort Sumter and

Lieutenant Hall was then to bring the women and children to the new fort.

That afternoon, Major Anderson told Captain Doubleday, "You have twenty minutes to get your company ready. We are moving our garrison to Fort Sumter."

"Yes sir!" Captain Doubleday snapped to attention and saluted.

Major Anderson was waiting with the garrison flag folded under his arm when Captains Doubleday and Seymour joined him with their companies. The major led his men to the old seawall where three boats were hidden behind the rocks. Major Anderson went with Lieutenant Snyder in the first boat. Lieutenant Meade followed in the second and Captain Doubleday was in charge of the third.

Captain John Foster was left at Fort Moultrie with five men. He was to watch with a telescope and if the patrol boats stopped Major Anderson he was to sink them with the cannon.

A full moon shone brightly as the boats quietly moved toward the dark fort. They were almost halfway across when they saw the first patrol boat, *Nina*. Major Anderson and

Lieutenant Meade made a wide circle toward Charleston around the stern and were not seen.

Captain Doubleday decided that with hard rowing he could go safely in front of the steamer. The men at the oars did their best, but Doubleday soon realized that they would be discovered. Quickly he removed his hat and opened his topcoat to hide the shiny buttons.

"Take off your coats and lay them over your guns so the moonlight won't reflect on them," he ordered. "Perhaps the captain of the patrol boat will think we are a party of laborers returning to Fort Sumter."

On the parapet at Fort Moultrie, Captain Foster held his breath as he watched the two boats come nearer together. He would fire if the patrol boat halted Captain Doubleday.

The paddle wheels of the *Nina* stopped. Captain Doubleday's men continued to row toward the fort. Then the wheels started again and the steamer went on its way.

When the three boats had reached the fort, Danny Sinclair heard the signal guns. The two boats with the women and children arrived safely at Fort Sumter a few minutes later.

Next morning the crew of the *Nina* rubbed their eyes in amazement when they saw the soldiers on the parapets of Fort Sumter. They hurried to Charleston to tell that Fort Sumter had been occupied by Union soldiers.

Governor Francis Pickens sent his aide to Fort Sumter to demand that Major Anderson return his men to Fort Moultrie. Major Anderson explained that Fort Moultrie was not safe.

"I am a Southerner," the major told the aide. "But I am an officer in the Army of the United States. My duty comes first."

As soon as the aide left, Major Anderson sent a boat to bring Chaplain Harris to the fort. The garrison was ordered to the parade and the major marched out carrying the folded flag. After the chaplain said a prayer, the flag was raised above the high walls of Fort Sumter. The band played "Hail Columbia" and the men cheered again and again.

In New York, Major Anderson's wife, Eliza, listened to the shouts of the people in the streets praising her husband. Although she had been in bed with a fever she decided she must go to see him. She found Sergeant Peter Hart, who had been Major Anderson's aide in the Mexican War, working as a policeman. He had heard what the major had done and was anxious to join him.

When they arrived in Charleston they were met by Eliza's brother and Major Anderson's brother. They received permission to go over to the fort but the governor said that Peter Hart could not remain as a soldier. He would have to be a civilian workman.

When they arrived at Fort Sumter, Major Anderson could hardly believe his eyes.

"We have bad news and good news," the major's brother told him. "Several other states are planning to join South Carolina to form a Confederacy. However, the House of Representatives in Washington has voted that you have done a patriotic act."

Governor Pickens called Major Anderson the enemy and announced that no supplies or food could be sent from Charleston to Fort Sumter.

President Buchanan received hundreds of letters demanding that reinforcements be sent to Major Anderson at once. Finally, he decided to send a warship with food and troops. General

Winfield Scott said that the Charlestonians would be angry if a warship were sent. So President Buchanan agreed to send an unarmed merchant ship, the *Star of the West*.

General Scott wrote Major Anderson that he should protect the *Star of the West* if she were fired on. No one knows what happened to that letter, but Major Anderson never received it.

The *Star of the West* arrived at Charleston Harbor early one morning. She was seen by a small patrol boat which signalled wildly with rockets to alert the Confederate forts.

In Fort Sumter Captain Doubleday sighted the ship. At his shout, Danny Sinclair ran with

the men to the parapets. Suddenly Danny saw a cannon shot arc over the bow of the merchant ship. The first shot of the War Between the States had been fired by a young Citadel cadet named George E. Haynsworth of Sumter, South Carolina; the boy was not much older than Danny himself.

Since Major Anderson had not received the letter from General Scott, he had no way of knowing that the merchant ship was bringing him reinforcements and that he was expected to protect her. He gave no order to fire.

The captain of the *Star of the West* held a hurried consultation with his officers. They

agreed that they could not get past Fort Moultrie without protection from Fort Sumter. The captain brought the ship around and started toward the open sea.

As the ship steamed away, the officers at Fort Sumter had to use all their authority to keep the men from firing on Fort Morris and Fort Moultrie without Major Anderson's order.

The next day the governor sent two aides to the fort. He demanded that Major Anderson hand over Fort Sumter to South Carolina.

"Shall we agree to the demands of the governor or not?" the major asked his officers.

Everyone voted against leaving.

Major Anderson turned to the governor's messengers. "We will fire the magazine and be burned with our fort before we shall surrender," he declared.

The men returned to the work of fortifying the fort. Danny helped make hand grenades by filling shells with powder. When they ran out of cloth for powder bags, Major Anderson donated all of his socks and the men sewed them with the fort's six needles.

Food and supplies were getting lower and lower. No matter how he tried, Danny's father could not buy food in Charleston. The men were on a diet of salt pork with half rations of coffee. Only a few lucky men had a little tobacco left. Candles and soap were almost gone.

Major Anderson was faced with another decision. The wives and children of the soldiers made forty-five more mouths to feed. The major wrote the governor for permission to send the women and children to New York.

Danny was near tears. "I can help do anything a soldier can do," he begged his friend, Captain Doubleday. "And I won't eat anything."

"You have been a brave boy, Danny," said the captain gruffly. "I wish you could stay, too. But your mother and brother will need you and we will just have to get along without you."

Danny tried not to cry while he helped his father with the luggage. As they steamed away from Fort Sumter the major honored them with a one-gun salute.

On March 1, Confederate Brigadier General Pierre Gustave Toutant Beauregard, recently of the United States Army, arrived in Charleston. Major Anderson had taught the new general at West Point and knew that he was brilliant. He would make a tough enemy.

When Abraham Lincoln was inaugurated on March 4 he said in his address: "My power as president will be used to hold, occupy and possess the property of the government . . ." Everyone knew that the new president would support Major Anderson at Fort Sumter.

Soon the major received word from the Secretary of War telling him that a fleet with reinforcements and supplies would be sent to him. The major replied that reinforcements would be of little use now that the South Carolinians had strengthened their forts around him. Major Anderson's reply never reached

Washington. It was delivered to General Beauregard instead.

The next day Major Anderson received a note from General Beauregard saying that no further mail would be allowed to go into or out of Fort Sumter. Three days later the general sent his aides to Fort Sumter. They handed a note to Major Anderson, who called his officers into his quarters.

"General Beauregard demands that we evacuate the fort," the major told them. "He says that we will not be taken prisoners but can go to any post in the United States that I may choose. We may salute our flag and take it with us."

"We'll never surrender," Captain Doubleday said vehemently.

"This would not be surrender," the major said. "We would evacuate the fort of our own free will."

"The terms are generous," said Lieutenant Meade. "General Beauregard knows we are starving and he has only to wait until we beg for mercy."

"Yes, he knows that," said Major Anderson. "And I must tell you that if we decide to remain here, there will be a fight and you may lose your lives. Now we will vote."

Every man voted to stay in Fort Sumter.

General Beauregard was upset by Major Anderson's refusal to evacuate the fort. He did not want to attack his former teacher. Also, it would take time to lay siege to the fort and he was afraid the reinforcements would arrive and he would have to fight them, also. Just after midnight he again sent his messengers to Fort Sumter. This time they were to ask if the major would set a date to evacuate the fort.

Major Anderson asked Dr. Crawford how long he thought the men could last and do any fighting.

"No more than five days," the doctor said.

The major wrote a reply saying that he would evacuate the fort in three days if it were not fired on in that time. This would allow the fleet to get there.

The aide read the note and shook his head. He also knew that the fleet could arrive in that time.

"I am instructed to reply for General Beauregard," he said. "We will open fire on Fort Sumter in one hour from this time."

As the Confederate forts opened fire, the news passed quickly through the city. Even before dawn many Charleston citizens went up onto the roofs of the houses along the battery to see the show.

As commander of the fort, Major Anderson could have fired the first gun. However, he was a Southerner and he did not feel that the Confederates were his enemies. He asked Captain Doubleday to fire it instead. Doubleday accepted eagerly. He believed the Southerners were traitors to the United States and that his side was right.

The Confederate guns were accurate and shells and cannonballs fell on Fort Sumter.

Early in the afternoon a shout came from the parapet.

"The fleet! The fleet!"

The men cheered at the sight of the *Baltic*, the *Pawnee* and the *Harriet Lane* flying the Stars and Stripes. All day the ships stood off the bar. The men in the fort did not expect them to run through the Confederate fire in daylight but talked of their arrival that night.

About dark it began to rain. Gale winds lashed the fort in a fierce storm. Major Anderson knew that he would receive no help from the ships in such a rough sea. The Confederate guns fired all night in spite of the storm and the brick walls of the fort began to crumble. At daybreak the weather cleared. The ships could still be seen off the bar but showed no sign of trying to enter the harbor. For the first time the men inside Fort Sumter were discouraged.

From all sides the bombardment began again. Red-hot balls set fire to the barracks and flames licked toward the powder magazine.

Suddenly, the flagstaff was broken by an enemy ball. Young Lieutenant Hall dashed onto the searing heat of the parade. His hair was

singed but he brought back the flag. Peter Hart found a long spar and climbed up the parapet where he raised the flag again in the face of enemy guns firing at him.

By 1:30 P.M. on Saturday, April 13, 1861, after thirty-three hours of bombardment, the flag that Peter Hart had raised was taken down and a hospital sheet was put in its place. Major Anderson knew that further fighting was useless.

As soon as General Beauregard saw the white flag, he sent his aides over to the fort. They were greeted by the major whose face was smudged with soot and his uniform burned from falling ash.

"I will evacuate the fort at once," he told them, "if the terms are the same as those to which I agreed the other day. Otherwise I will run up my flag again and continue the fight."

The Confederate officers looked around the burning fort with admiration for Major Anderson and his men. Then they returned to General Beauregard with the message. The general was ready to accept but Governor Pickens said that Major Anderson could not salute his flag as it was lowered. He must surrender.

When the aides returned to the fort with this reply, the major refused it. He would not surrender. He would leave with the full honors of war or not at all.

Finally, Governor Pickens agreed, and that night the men packed what few possessions were left. Not one human being had been killed or wounded during the bombardment.

At noon on Sunday the garrison at Fort Sumter formed in full uniform. As the cannon boomed in salute, Peter Hart lowered the tattered flag.

Even though half destroyed, Fort Sumter was useful in the long war that followed. It kept Charleston Harbor open so that Confederate war supplies could be brought in and cotton shipped out to pay for them. The Confederates started work immediately to rebuild the fort and by June, 1862, it was almost completed.

When the new little ironclad Union ship, *Monitor*, defeated the Confederate ship, *Merrimac*, at Hampton Roads, Virginia, the United States Navy decided that it could take Fort Sumter with battleships. On April 5, 1863, Admiral Dahlgren led a fleet of nine Union ironclad ships, armed with the heaviest guns ever used in war, into Charleston Harbor. They steamed up the main channel toward Fort Sumter and for the next two and one-half hours the battle raged. Only thirty-four rounds hit the fort and it remained strong and secure. The North was stunned at this failure. They must now lay siege to the fort.

Colonel Alfred Rhett, who was in charge of the garrison at Fort Sumter, prepared for the siege. Thousands of sandbags were stacked against the walls and the rooms were filled with damp cotton bales.

On the morning of July 10, General Truman Seymour, who had been a captain at Fort Sum-

ter when it was evacuated two years before, led three thousand Union infantrymen to attack Morris Island. Within four hours they had taken three-fourths of the island, but the Confederate forces continued to hold Fort Wagner. The next day the 54th Massachusetts Regiment, the first regiment to be made up entirely of Negroes, attacked Fort Wagner, but the Confederates held on.

Aided by Admiral Dahlgren and his fleet, General Seymour attacked Fort Sumter. For twenty-one days they besieged the fort and it was once again crushed to a pile of rubble. Admiral Dahlgren demanded the fort's surrender but General Beauregard replied: "The admiral can have Fort Sumter when he can take it and hold it."

A few nights later the admiral tried to do just that. He sent four hundred sailors and marines in small boats to land at Fort Sumter. The Confederate garrison coolly held their fire until the men began to land. Then they let loose with musket fire, hand grenades, fire balls, brickbats, and pieces of masonry. It was all over in twenty minutes. One hundred and twenty-four Union men were killed, wounded, and captured. Five boats were taken.

For nineteen days after the landing failure, Fort Sumter was free from attack. On October 26 the bombardment began again. Night and day the Union guns kept up a steady fire on the fort. Still, the Confederates remained snug in the ruins.

After forty-one days the firing stopped. The Union naval and land troops were needed elsewhere. Again Fort Sumter was repaired, but this time there was neither money nor man-power to rebuild.

General J.G. Foster, who had been the engineer at Fort Sumter when Major Anderson held it, made the last attack on the fort. He built special steamers with elevated towers for sharpshooters and tall scaling ladders. On July 7, 1864, he attacked with the heaviest bombardment Fort Sumter had yet received. At one point the walls were destroyed to only twenty feet above high tide.

General Foster's ammunition grew lower and during the autumn of 1864 he could defend only Morris Island. Fort Sumter had won again.

In February of 1865 General Sherman began his march from Savannah through South Carolina. When he reached Columbia, the South Carolinians knew that they were beaten. They quietly evacuated Fort Sumter. Once more the Stars and Stripes were raised over the fort that had never been surrendered.

With the war at an end, President Lincoln decided that there should be a special anniversary celebration of the evacuation of Fort Sumter by Major Anderson, now General Anderson. He would raise again the old flag that he had taken with him and kept all these years.

At the fort a large wooden platform was built over the rubble in the parade. It was covered with a canopy and surrounded by stands to seat four thousand spectators. The seats were already filled and many people were standing when General Anderson arrived.

Peter Hart followed, carrying the flag. General Doubleday and several of the other officers sat on the front row as Chaplain Matthias Harris said a prayer. Then Peter Hart raised the flag and the spectators leaped to their feet and cheered him.

General Anderson took hold of the halyards.

"Glory to God in the highest," he said, "and on earth peace, good will towards men."

That night, at a dinner in the Charleston Hotel, General Anderson offered a toast to the President of the United States. Less than an hour after the toast was drunk, President Lincoln lay dying in Washington with a bullet in his brain.

In the 1870's the rubble and ruin of war were cleared from the interior of Fort Sumter and the work of reconstruction began. The outer walls were partly rebuilt, but in 1876 there was no more money and the work stopped. For the next twenty-three years the fort was used as a lighthouse station with only one man in charge.

During World War II Fort Sumter was armed with 90-millimeter anti-aircraft guns which were manned by a garrison of Coast Artillery.

In 1948 Congress made Fort Sumter a national monument. It is now administered by the National Park Service. Every year thousands of school children and adult visitors take a boat across Charleston Harbor to see the remains of the fort in which men on both sides fought gallantly for what they believed was right in the War Between the States.

31

ABOUT THE AUTHOR:
   Eugenia Burney was born in Orangeburg, South Carolina, just seventy miles from Fort Sumter, where she often visited as a child. She attended the University of South Carolina where she started her journalistic career. She has been an editor of books, magazines, and newspapers. After helping her husband, Gardell Dano Christensen, with his books for ten years, she has now written two children's books of her own. Now retired, Eugenia is devoting all her time to writing. She lives with her husband on a big farm near Savannah, Georgia.

ABOUT THE ARTIST:
   Chuck Mitchell is a Chicago artist who specializes in editorial and book illustration.